Nature's MATHEMATICAL MARVELS

CONTENTS

JAMES BURNETT
CALVIN IRONS

D1209357

SOMEWHERE IN SPACE

Earth, the planet that is our home, is one of nine planets that travel around the sun. This whole *solar system* is a tiny part of a galaxy known as the Milky Way – just one of many billions of galaxies that make up the universe.

The sun in this picture looks smaller than the planets, but actually it is much, much bigger. Its diameter is 865,000 miles – more than one hundred times the diameter of the earth.

Orbits

The nine planets in the solar system all revolve around, or *orbit,* the sun. The farther away from the sun a planet is, the longer one orbit takes.

Planets	Number of days to orbit the sun
Mercury	88
Venus	225
Earth	365
Mars	687
Jupiter	4,329
Saturn	10,753
Uranus	30,664
Neptune	60,158
Pluto	90,411

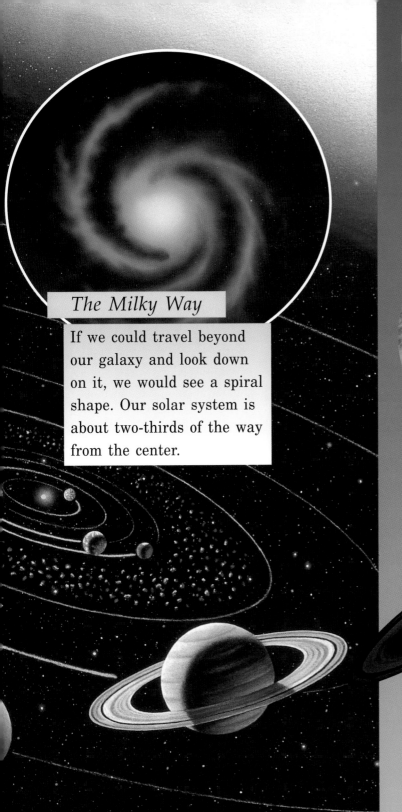

The Milky Way

If we could travel beyond our galaxy and look down on it, we would see a spiral shape. Our solar system is about two-thirds of the way from the center.

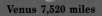

Mercury 3,031 miles

Venus 7,520 miles

Earth 7,926 miles

Mars 4,217 miles

Jupiter 88,846 miles

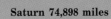

Saturn 74,898 miles

Uranus 31,763 miles

Neptune 30,775 miles

Pluto 1,419 miles

3

A WATERY WORLD

Earth provides many different landscapes: forests, deserts, mountain ranges, valleys, and plains. However, most of the earth's surface is covered by water.

Did you know?
More than 0.97 of all our planet's water is in the oceans and seas. A small fraction of the earth's water (0.02) is ice, and the remainder is in lakes and rivers, underground, or in the atmosphere.

Research

- Find out the distance around the equator (the earth's *circumference*). How does this distance compare to the earth's diameter?

- Pluto was the last planet in our solar system to be discovered. Find out how long ago it was found.

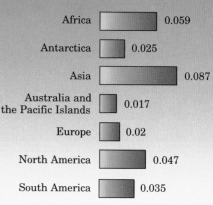

Fractions of the earth covered by land

Africa	0.059
Antarctica	0.025
Asia	0.087
Australia and the Pacific Islands	0.017
Europe	0.02
North America	0.047
South America	0.035

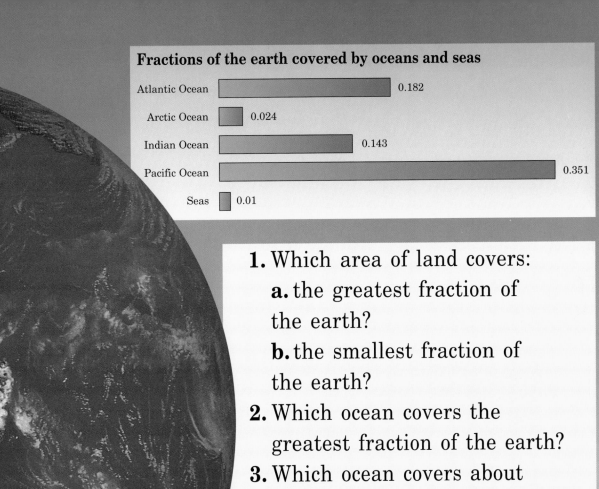

Fractions of the earth covered by oceans and seas

Atlantic Ocean	0.182
Arctic Ocean	0.024
Indian Ocean	0.143
Pacific Ocean	0.351
Seas	0.01

1. Which area of land covers:
   a. the greatest fraction of the earth?
   b. the smallest fraction of the earth?
2. Which ocean covers the greatest fraction of the earth?
3. Which ocean covers about one-third of the earth?
4. Which land area covers about half as much of the earth as the Atlantic Ocean?
5. Write all the land areas *and* oceans and seas in order from largest to smallest.
6. What fraction of the earth:
   a. does all the land cover?
   b. do all the oceans and seas cover?
   What happens when you add these two fractions?

MIGHTY MOUNTAINS

On land and below the sea, the earth's surface is a very uneven place. In some areas it dips steeply in valleys and trenches; in others, rugged mountain ranges rise tens of thousands of feet toward the sky.

Mount Aconcagua
22,834 feet

Mount Kilimanjaro
19,340 feet

Mont Blanc
15,770 feet

The illustration shows each continent's highest mountain and its height above sea level. The map below shows each mountain's location.

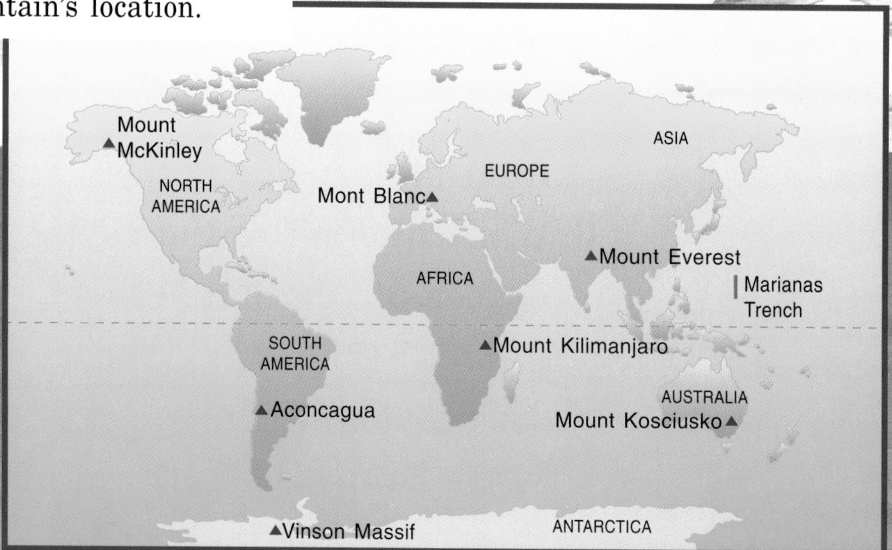

Mount Kosciusk
7,314 fe

Mount McKinley

NORTH AMERICA

Mont Blanc

EUROPE

ASIA

AFRICA

Mount Everest

Marianas Trench

SOUTH AMERICA

Mount Kilimanjaro

Aconcagua

AUSTRALIA

Mount Kosciusko

Vinson Massif

ANTARCTICA

Under the sea
The world's tallest mountain is *not* one of the seven shown below. Mauna Kea, in Hawaii, is an awesome 33,480 feet tall – but 19,684 feet of this is hidden below sea level.

Sea level

33,480 feet

Mount Everest
29,022 feet

Mount McKinley
20,320 feet

Vinson Massif
16,066 feet

Did you know?
The depth of some ocean trenches is greater than the height of many mountains. The Marianas trench in the Pacific goes down 35,837 feet at its deepest point. How does this compare to the height of Mt. Everest?

Empire State Building

In the whole world, 109 mountain peaks are higher than 24,000 feet. Ninety-six of these, including Mt. Everest, are in the great mountain range known as the Himalayas.

7

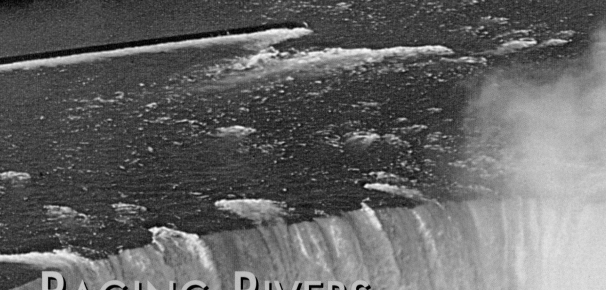

RAGING RIVERS

All over the world, rivers wind their way to the sea. For some rivers, it is a journey of thousands of miles.

The longest rivers of six continents:

The Amazon
(SOUTH AMERICA)
4,007 miles

The Mississippi River System
(NORTH AMERICA)
3,710 miles

The Danube
(EUROPE)
1,766 miles

The Murray River System
(AUSTRALIA)
2,330 miles

The Yangtze-Kiang
(ASIA)
3,915 miles

The Nile
(AFRICA)
4,145 miles

Amazing Amazon

The Amazon is a vast river system. If it ran through the United States, its "veins" would stretch across almost the whole country!

Although the Amazon is shorter than the Nile, it carries 60 times more water to its mouth. In fact, in one day the Amazon carries more fresh water than the next eight longest rivers combined – enough water to supply every home in the United States.

1. What is the world's longest river? How much shorter than this is the Mississippi?

2. The distance between San Francisco and New York is about 2,550 miles.
   How much longer than this is:
   a. the Nile?
   b. the Amazon?
   c. the Yangtze-Kiang?

Look at the mountains on pages 6–7.

3. One mile is 5,280 feet. Which mountain is closest to:
   a. 3 miles high?   **b.** 4 miles high?
   Explain how you found the answers.

4. If a mountain was 10 miles high, how much taller than Mt. Everest would it be?

5. How far above sea level is the peak of Mauna Kea?

GOING TO EXTREMES

The weather is constantly changing. Conditions vary greatly from one part of the world to another – and sometimes from one hour to the next!

Coldest

Vostok Base in Antarctica is the coldest place on earth. The world's lowest temperature, −128.6°F, was recorded there on July 21, 1983.

Hot to cold

The greatest temperature drop in a 24-hour period occurred in January, 1916, in Browning, Montana. The temperature fell from 44°F to −56°F!

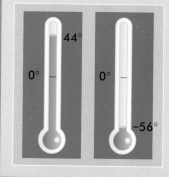

Deepest snowfall

The greatest snowfall in a 24-hour period occurred in April, 1921, when 75 inches of snow fell at Silver Lake, Colorado.

Fastest wind
Winds of 280 miles per hour were recorded on April 2, 1958, as a tornado swept across Wichita Falls, Texas.

Hottest
The highest temperature ever recorded is 136.4°F. It occurred on September 13, 1992, at Al Aziziyah in Libya, North Africa.

Cold to hot
On a January morning in 1943, the temperature suddenly skyrocketed at Spearfish, South Dakota. In two minutes it rose 49°, from −4°F to 45°F.

Driest
The driest place in the world is the Atacama Desert, in Chile, South America. It receives less than $\frac{1}{250}$ of an inch of rain each year.

WET, WET, WET

Some places have frequent rain nearly all year round, while some have almost no rain at any time. In other places, a particular part of the year is the "rainy season."

Darwin, Australia

(Rainfall in inches: Jan., Feb., Mar., Apr., May, June, July, Aug., Sep., Oct., Nov., Dec.)

Research

- Find out some record weather conditions for your town. Record your data in a chart.
- Find out how much rain your town received each month last year. Construct a bar graph to show the data. Did your town receive more rain before or after the end of June?

These bar graphs show how many inches of rain fell in two different cities in the same year.

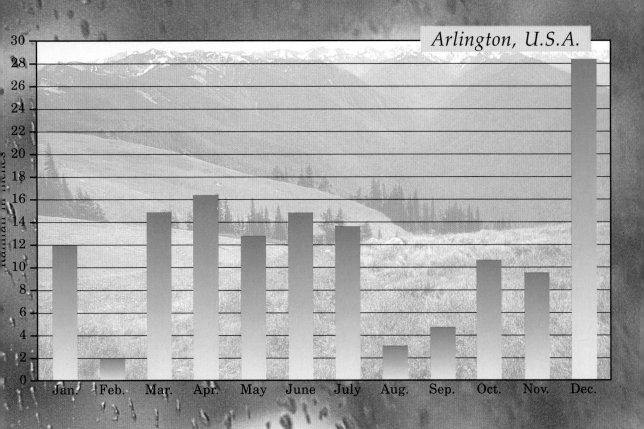

Arlington, U.S.A.

Rainfall in inches

Jan. Feb. Mar. Apr. May June July Aug. Sep. Oct. Nov. Dec.

Look at the bar graphs.

1. When did both locations receive:
   a. more than 18 inches of rain in the same month?
   b. less than 10 inches of rain in the same month?
2. How many months of the year had less than two inches of rain:
   a. in Darwin?   **b.** in Arlington?
3. Which place had the greater increase in rainfall between November and December?
4. Which location received more rain for the whole year? How could you tell?

Record Rain
- On one day in March, 1952, an island in the Indian Ocean received $73\frac{1}{2}$ inches of rain. This is the greatest rainfall ever recorded in a 24-hour period.
- Mount Wai-ále-ále in Hawaii records more rainy days than anywhere else in the world. It has rain on as many as 350 days per year.

GROWING UP

All living things grow, and in the plant kingdom, some grow to amazing sizes. The world's tallest trees reach higher than a 30-story building!

Tree Tops

This graph shows the five tallest trees ever recorded. They are not all still standing.

Height in feet

| 450 | 400 | 350 | 300 | 250 | 200 | 150 | 100 | 50 | 0 |

Mountain Ash, Victoria, Australia
Coast Redwood, California, U.S.A.
Coast Douglas Fir, Oregon, U.S.A.
Giant Sequoia, California, U.S.A.
Noble Fir, Washington, U.S.A.

The tree that has the nick-name "General Sherman" is a 3,500 year old giant sequoia in California. It measures 102 feet around its base.

The largest leaf ever recorded had a surface area of 34 square feet. It was found in Malaysia.

The world's tallest recorded tree was measured at 435 feet, but the top may have broken off. At one time it might have been 500 feet tall.

Growing Fast

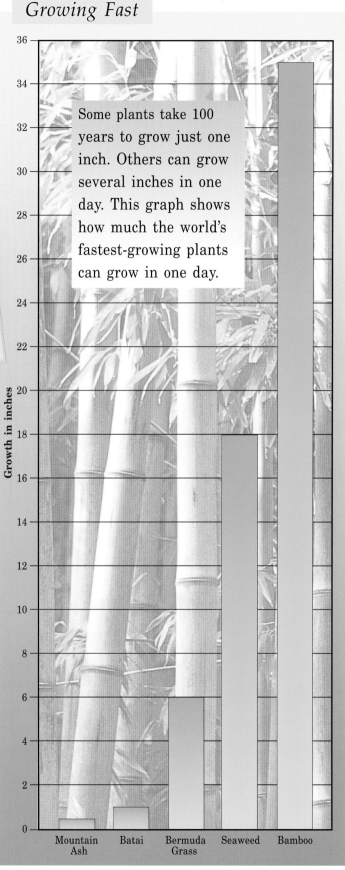

Some plants take 100 years to grow just one inch. Others can grow several inches in one day. This graph shows how much the world's fastest-growing plants can grow in one day.

Growth in inches

Mountain Ash | Batai | Bermuda Grass | Seaweed | Bamboo

NATURE'S NUMBERS

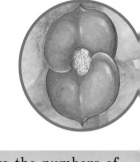

Have you ever tried to find a four-leaf clover? Four is not an easy number to find in plants of any kind – but certain other numbers appear very often.

A Branching Pattern

As a stem on a plant grows longer, it can produce another stem just like itself.

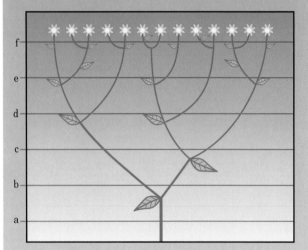

Look along each red line on this "Branching Pattern" illustration (lines a-f). Count the number of stems the plant has at each line. What pattern do you notice?

R esearch

- Find out the height of a tall tree in your area. How does the height of this tree compare to the trees on page 14?

Many flowers have the numbers of petals shown in these illustrations. The first flower has two petals; the next has three; the next has five . . . Count the others for yourself and see what you find.

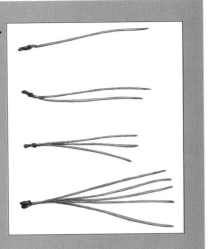

Pine needles grow in clusters. The number of needles in a cluster varies, but it is always a number in the sequence 1, 2, 3, 5, 8, and so on. Numbers from this sequence, in which each number is the sum of the previous two numbers, are often found in nature.

1. Make a list of the number of petals on each flower, starting with the smallest number.

   a. What do you notice about the numbers? Write about a pattern you see.

   b. There are flowers that have many more petals than the flowers shown. Predict how many petals the next two flowers in the sequence might have. Explain your answer.

2. Look at the graph on page 15. Make a chart to show how much each plant would grow in:

   a. two days　　**b.** one week.

3. Look at the picture graph on page 14. Using the data, write your own question about the giant trees.

BEAUTIFUL BALANCE

Many objects made by people have lines of balance or symmetry. But some of the most stunning examples of *line symmetry* occur in nature's living things.

Most animal faces are symmetrical in shape. In some animals, markings are in a balanced pattern as well.

Objects with a *line of symmetry* have halves that are mirror images of each other. Each of these flowers and creatures is balanced in this way.

LEAFY LINES

Leaves appear in thousands of different shapes and sizes, yet almost every leaf has some lines of balance or symmetry.

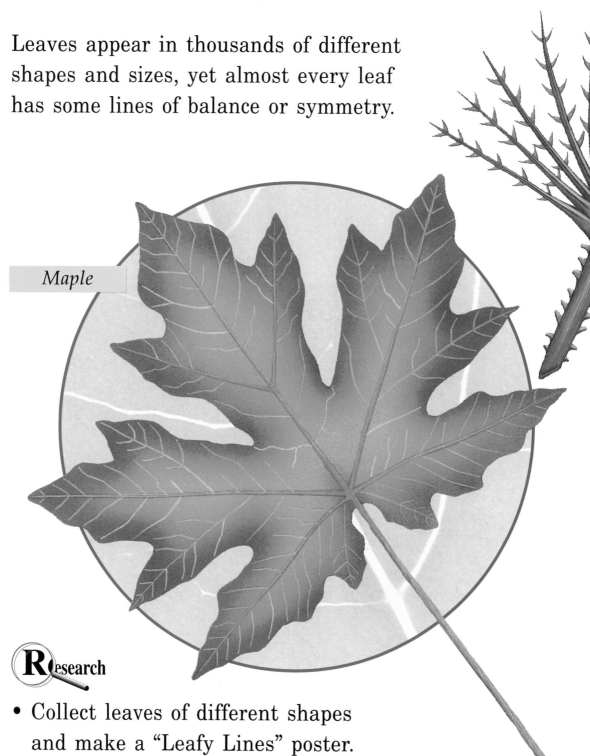

Maple

Research

• Collect leaves of different shapes and make a "Leafy Lines" poster. Mark the leaves' lines of symmetry.

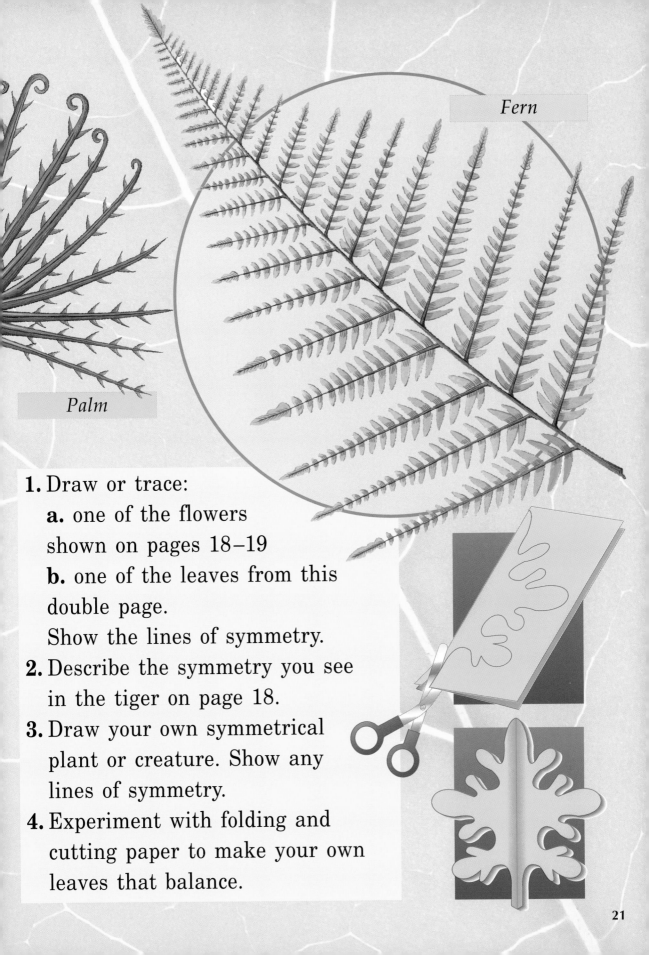

Fern

Palm

1. Draw or trace:
   a. one of the flowers shown on pages 18–19
   b. one of the leaves from this double page.
   Show the lines of symmetry.

2. Describe the symmetry you see in the tiger on page 18.

3. Draw your own symmetrical plant or creature. Show any lines of symmetry.

4. Experiment with folding and cutting paper to make your own leaves that balance.

PERFECT FIT

Some shapes can fit together like tiles, without leaving any gaps. These are known as shapes that *tessellate*. In nature they are seen in many different places.

Beehive
Bees build their honeycomb hives using hexagons of equal size.

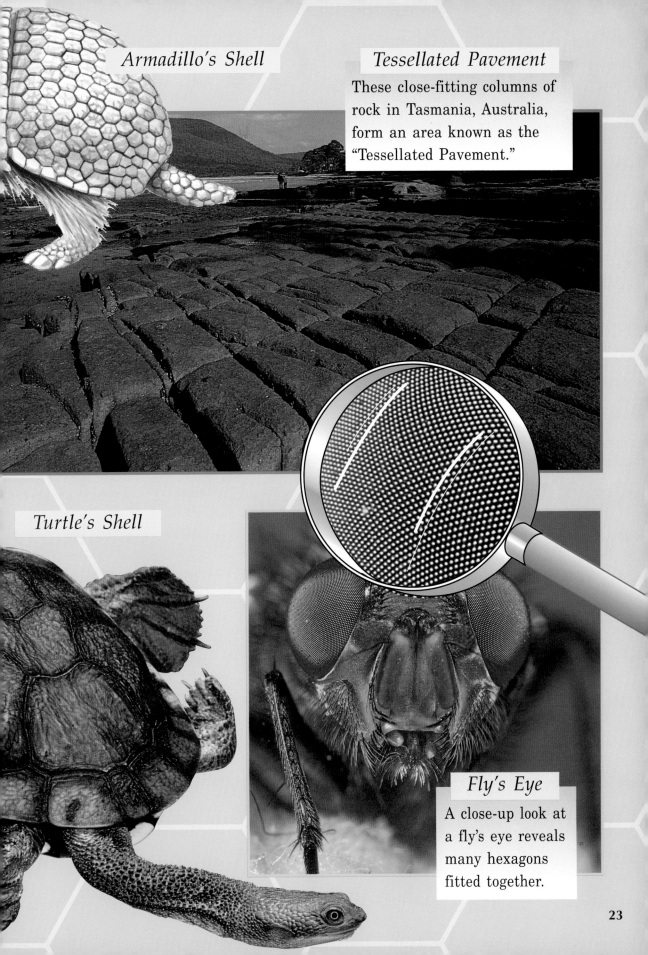

Armadillo's Shell

Tessellated Pavement

These close-fitting columns of rock in Tasmania, Australia, form an area known as the "Tessellated Pavement."

Turtle's Shell

Fly's Eye

A close-up look at a fly's eye reveals many hexagons fitted together.

FILLING THE GAPS

The shapes in a beehive are hexagons. Like some other regular shapes, hexagons repeated at the same size over and over again can be used to cover areas of many different shapes and sizes.

Regular Polygons

A polygon is a straight-sided flat shape with three or more sides. In a regular polygon, all sides are equal and all angles are equal.
For example:

- equilateral triangle
- square
- regular pentagon
- regular hexagon
- regular octagon

Only three regular polygons tessellate on their own.

1. **Experiment to find out which three regular polygons tessellate on their own.**
2. **A regular octagon will tessellate with one other regular polygon. Find out which shape is the octagon's tessellating partner.**
3. **Many different shapes can tessellate. Follow the steps on page 25 to create your own tessellation using a new shape.**

A New Shape

You will need:

a piece of heavy paper, at least 6 × 6 inches; construction paper; scissors; compass; tape.

Step 1: Follow steps 1 and 2 on page 29 to construct a large hexagon from heavy paper.

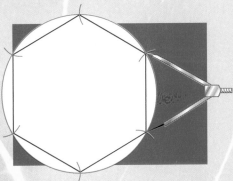

Step 2: Cut out a piece from one side of the hexagon.

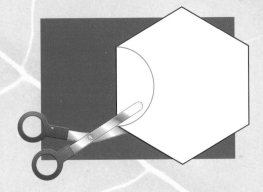

Step 3: Slide the piece straight across to the other side of the hexagon. Then reattach it using tape.

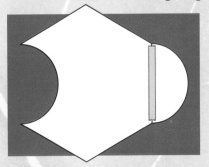

Step 4: Trace around your new shape to show a tessellating pattern.

AROUND AND AROUND

Some things in nature have "turning symmetry."
This means that they can be turned part way
around and still look exactly the same as before.

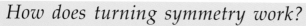

How does turning symmetry work?

This two-petaled flower
has turning symmetry.
You could turn it half way
around, and it would still
look exactly the same.

 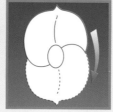

To start.   Half a turn later.

a

These flowers have
different numbers
of petals. Each one
needs to be rotated
a different fraction
of a turn to show
its symmetry.

b

c

Cut across the center,
an apple reveals a
five-pointed core that
has turning symmetry.

26

A Sea Urchin

A Jellyfish

A Starfish

FANCY FLAKES

Snowflakes provide some of the most beautiful examples of turning symmetry. Many snowflakes have this feature – even though the exact pattern of every snowflake is different.

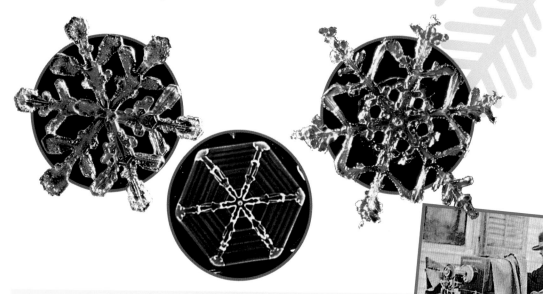

Look at flowers a, b, and c on page 26.

1. What fraction of a turn do you need to rotate each flower so it still looks the same?

2. What fraction of a turn do you need to rotate each of these so they still look the same?
   a. the jellyfish
   b. the starfish
   c. snowflakes.

3. Which flower is similar to the starfish? Explain how it is similar.

Some of the first photographs of snowflakes were taken early this century by Mr. W. Bentley. He photographed more than 6,000 snowflakes, and more than 2,000 were shown in his famous book, *Snow Crystals,* in 1931.

A Paper Snowflake

You will need:

white paper; a compass; scissors.

Step 1: Draw and cut out a circle. Then make six marks at even spaces around the edge.

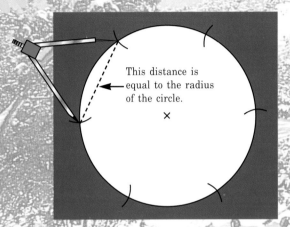

This distance is equal to the radius of the circle.

Step 2: Connect the points to make a hexagon. Cut out the new shape.

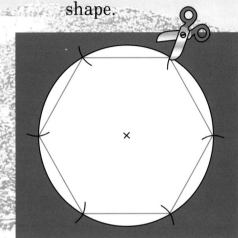

Step 3: a) Fold the shape in half. b) Fold the new shape in thirds.
c) Fold that shape in half again.

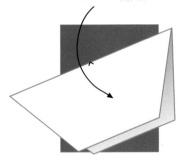
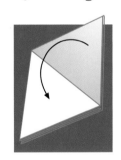
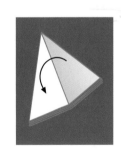

Step 4: Cut out an interesting shape. Be creative!

Step 5: Unfold your paper snowflake.

29

Natural Cycles

The intervals of time that we call a day, a month, and a year are all based on natural events that occur over and over again, or in *cycles*. For thousands of years, people have observed these cycles and used them to help organize their lives.

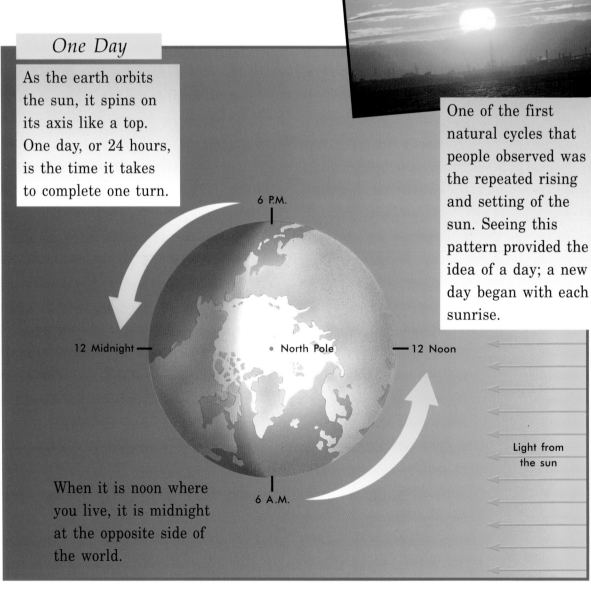

One Day

As the earth orbits the sun, it spins on its axis like a top. One day, or 24 hours, is the time it takes to complete one turn.

One of the first natural cycles that people observed was the repeated rising and setting of the sun. Seeing this pattern provided the idea of a day; a new day began with each sunrise.

6 P.M.

12 Midnight

North Pole

12 Noon

Light from the sun

6 A.M.

When it is noon where you live, it is midnight at the opposite side of the world.

One Month

The moon travels around the earth, completing one orbit in approximately $29\frac{1}{2}$ days. This cycle, which we can observe as the time from one full moon to the next, is called a *lunar month*.

The moon receives light from the sun. As the moon moves around the earth, we see different amounts of the lighted part.

One Year

A year is the length of time the earth takes to complete one orbit of the sun. One year is 365 days, 5 hours, 48 minutes, and 46 seconds long.

SUN AND SEASONS

Every day is 24 hours long, no matter what part of the world you are in or what time of year it is. However, the period of sunlight in a day varies greatly. In some parts of the world, there are summer days when the sun never sets.

Earth's Seasons

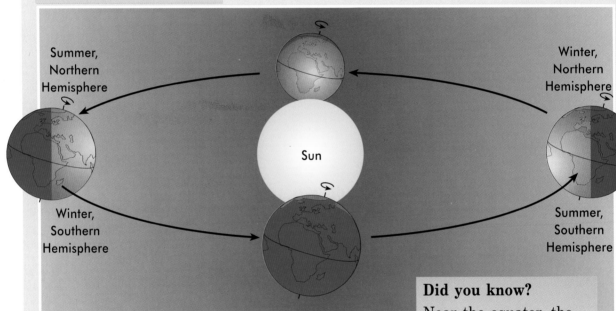

Summer, Northern Hemisphere

Winter, Northern Hemisphere

Sun

Winter, Southern Hemisphere

Summer, Southern Hemisphere

The amount of sunlight in a day varies through the year because of the way the earth tilts as it orbits the sun. This tilt also creates the seasons. Summer occurs when your hemisphere is tilted *toward* the sun; winter occurs when your part of the world is tilted *away* from the sun.

Did you know?
Near the equator, the period of daylight each day does not vary greatly from one season to another. As you go farther north or south, summer days stay light for longer, and winter days have less light.

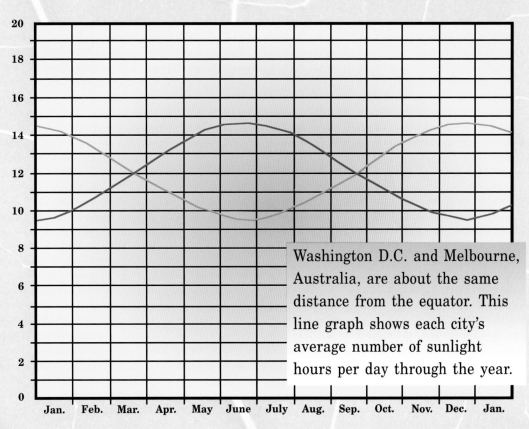

Average number of hours of sunlight each day.

Washington D.C. and Melbourne, Australia, are about the same distance from the equator. This line graph shows each city's average number of sunlight hours per day through the year.

Look at the line graph.

1. In which months do both cities have the same average number of sunlight hours?

2. Calculate the difference between the cities' sunlight hours in:
   a. mid-December **b.** mid-June.

Look at the information on pages 30–31.

3. About how many times does the earth rotate on its axis during one full orbit of the sun?

4. Calculate the exact number of days, hours, minutes, and seconds in:
   a. 2 years **b.** 3 years **c.** 4 years.

BUILT BIG!

Giants don't only exist in stories. Earth is home to many colossal creatures – some living in the sea, and some on land. The tallest animals tower above us, at more than three times the height of an adult human being!

African Giraffe

The tallest animal in the world, the African giraffe, can grow taller than 16 feet. The tallest on record stood close to 20 feet!

Giant Squid

The giant squid, the world's largest invertebrate (an animal without a backbone) measures up to 66 feet in length. This giant's eyes are bigger than those of any other animal; they can measure up to 20 inches in diameter.

African Elephant

The African elephant is the largest land animal, weighing in at as much as 7 tons and standing up to 11 feet tall.

Blue Whale

Blue whales are the world's largest animals. Measuring up to 91 feet in length and weighing about 145 tons, they dwarf most fishing boats.

African Ostrich

The world's largest bird is the North African ostrich. Males of this species stand up to 9 feet tall, and weigh as much as 345 pounds.

STYLED FOR SPEED

Animals vary greatly in size, and they also vary greatly in speed. Humans are not the slowest, by any means, but many creatures are much faster.

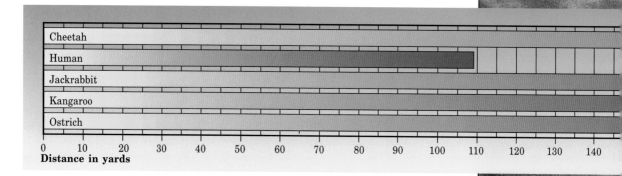

	Distance in yards
Cheetah	
Human	
Jackrabbit	
Kangaroo	
Ostrich	

0 10 20 30 40 50 60 70 80 90 100 110 120 130 140
Distance in yards

1. Which animal can run about twice as far in 10 seconds as a human?

2. If a cheetah could continue to run at top speed, how far would it travel in:
   a. 30 seconds?
   b. 1 minute?
   c. 10 minutes?

3. Estimate how far the following animals could travel in 10 seconds:
   a. an antelope that can run 1,616 yards in one minute
   b. a giant tortoise that can travel 298 yards in one minute.
   Show how you found your answers.

How Far in 10 Seconds at Top Speed?

| | | | | | | | | | | | | | | |
|160|170|180|190|200|210|220|230|240|250|260|270|280|290|300|

How Many Hops?

Some kangaroos can cover distances of up to 42 feet in a single bound. If a kangaroo kept jumping like that, how many times would it touch the ground in 100 yards?

With a top speed of 60 miles per hour, the cheetah is the fastest land animal.

Research

- Find out the record times for these Olympic track events:
  a. 100 meters   **b.** 200 meters
  c. 400 meters   **d.** 800 meters.
- How do the distances of these events compare?
- Compare the record times for each event. Which record-breaking runner ran fastest? How can you tell?

37

INSECT ATHLETICS

Most insects are small, but when it comes to physical performance, these little creatures are hard to beat.

Flex Those Muscles

The leg muscles of locusts are extremely powerful. A locust can jump about 10 times its own body length – from a standstill.

The High Jumpers

Fleas are the greatest jumpers in the animal kingdom. They can leap 130 times their own height.

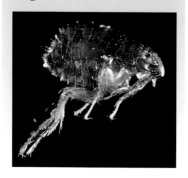

Champion Weight Lifter

Ants are among the strongest animals in the world. Some can lift up to 50 times their own body weight.

Distance Flyers

A honey bee can travel more than one mile from the hive in one day – not bad for an insect that is less than one inch long.

How many kinds of insects?

There are more than 30 million kinds or *species* of insects, including four kinds of honey bee and more than 4,000 kinds of dragonfly. The graph shows numbers of species for just a few members of the insect world.

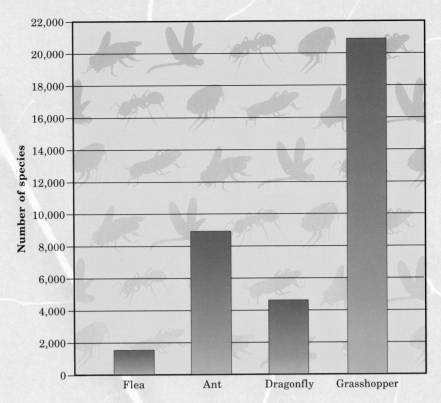

Super Speeds

Very few insects can fly faster than dragonflies. In short bursts, a dragonfly can reach 24 miles per hour.

1. How much weight could you lift if you could lift like an ant?
2. How high could you jump if you could jump like a flea?
3. Estimate the length of a locust that could jump 20 inches.
4. Look at the graph. Which insect has more than 10 times as many species as the flea? What other interesting data can you see in the graph?

Research

- Find out the distances that a frog, a kangaroo, and a human can "long jump." Organize your data into a graph.

CREEPY CRAWLIES

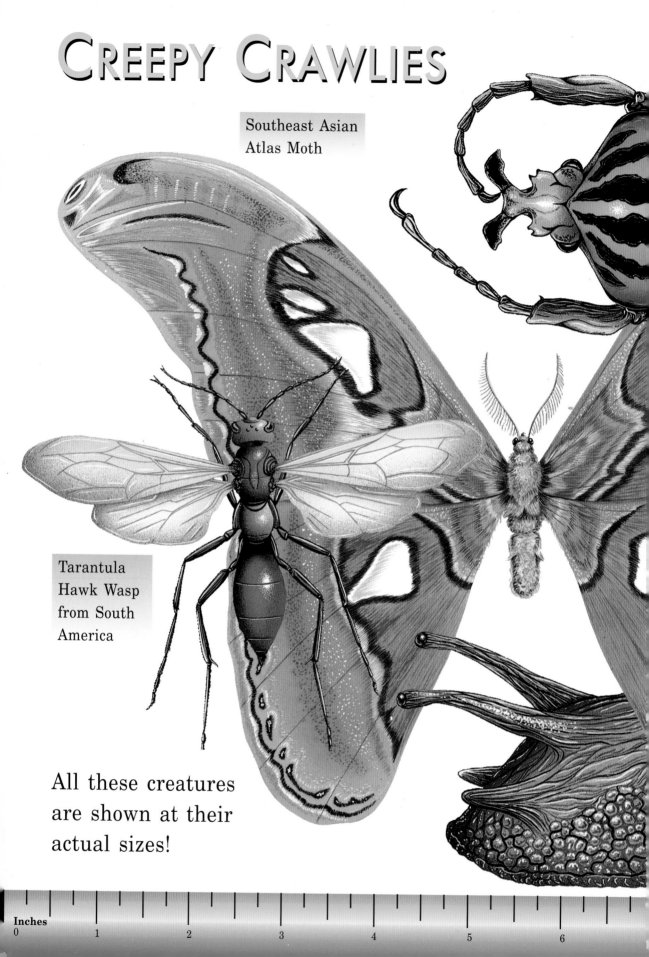

Southeast Asian
Atlas Moth

Tarantula
Hawk Wasp
from South
America

All these creatures
are shown at their
actual sizes!

Inches
0   1   2   3   4   5   6